Florida
ABC Coloring Book
An ABC Learning Activity Book all about Florida
With Count-to-10 Coloring Bonus!

Little Red Hills

Written & designed by: Rianna M. Hill

My ABCs Florida Coloring Book

name:

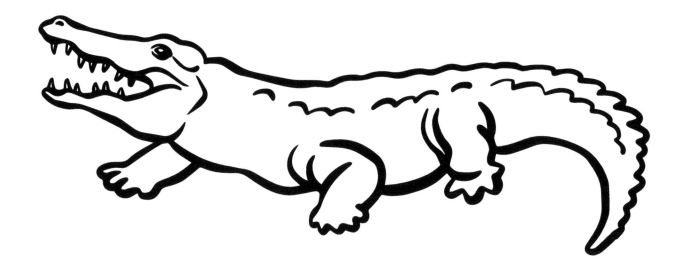

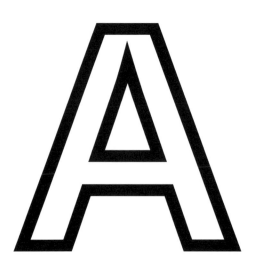

Alligator

Alligators are large reptiles and apex predators that are native to Florida's freshwater habitats. They are easily recognized by broad snouts and armored bodies.

B

Bottlenose
dolphin

Florida's coastal waters are inhabited by bottlenose dolphins. They're highly intelligent marine mammals often spotted in bays, estuaries, and the Gulf of Mexico.

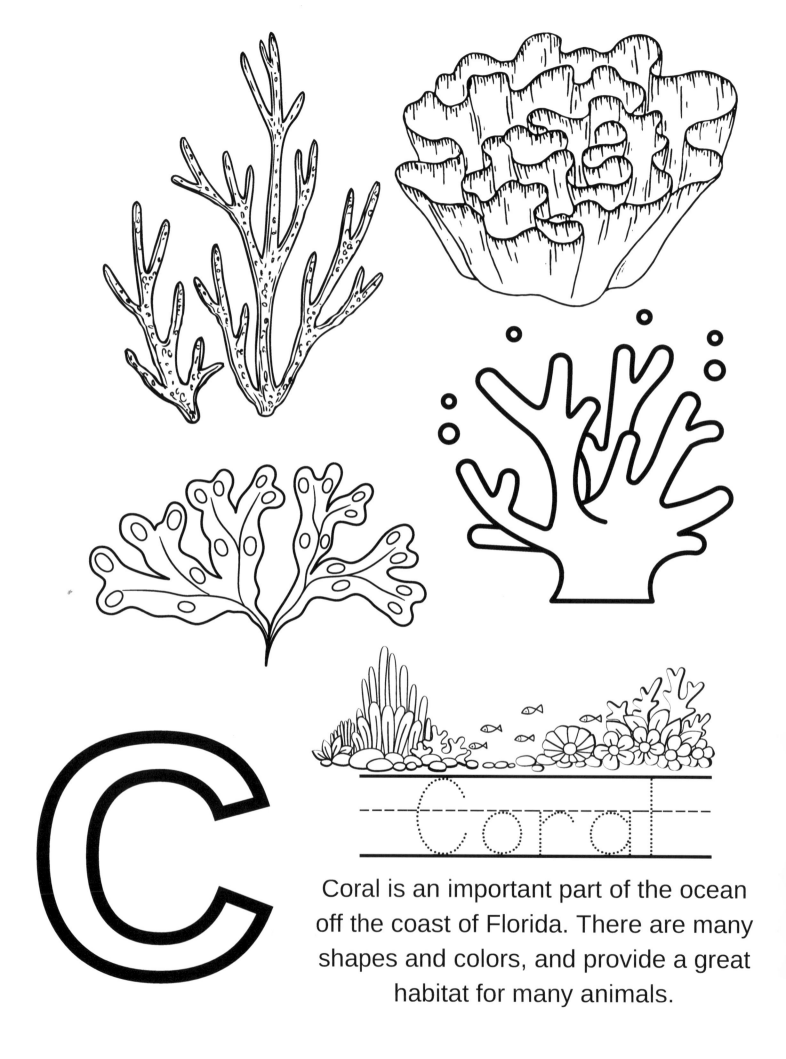

C Coral

Coral is an important part of the ocean off the coast of Florida. There are many shapes and colors, and provide a great habitat for many animals.

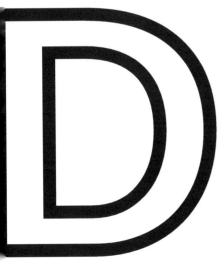 Disney World ™

In Orlando, this iconic place has four main theme parks, including the Animal Kingdom. There are many hotels, and people can travel around on the Magical Express.

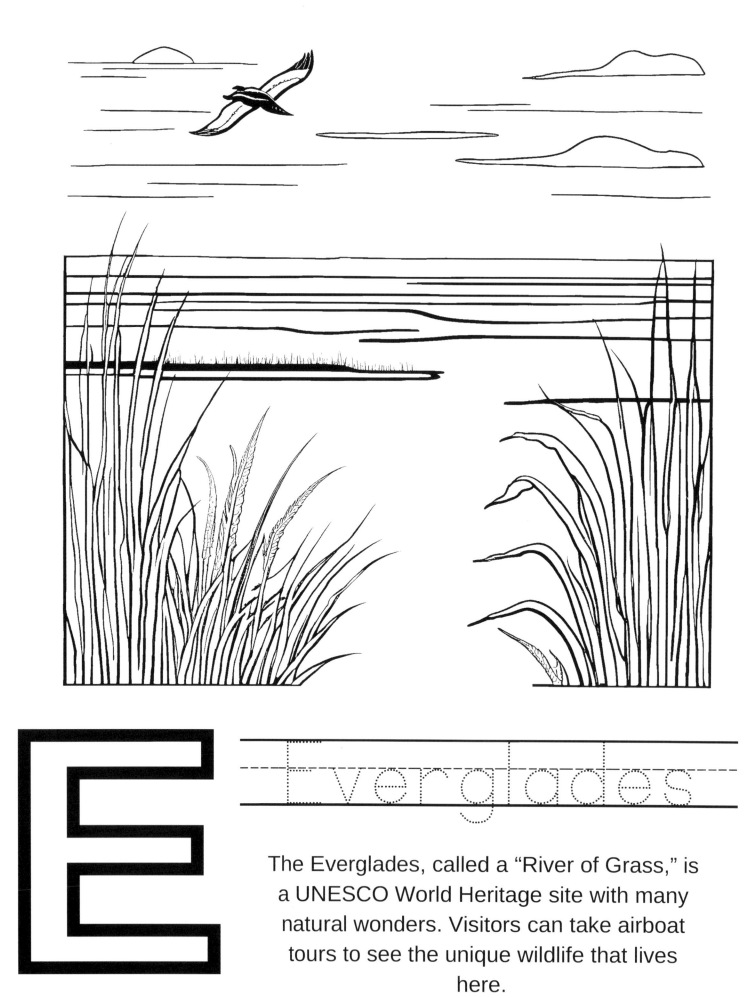

E

Everglades

The Everglades, called a "River of Grass," is a UNESCO World Heritage site with many natural wonders. Visitors can take airboat tours to see the unique wildlife that lives here.

F

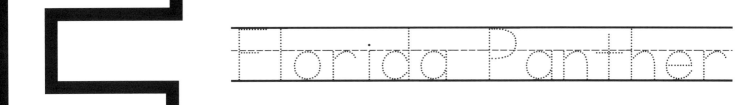

The Florida panther is a critically endangered species and the official state animal of Florida. These large, elusive cats primarily inhabit the southern part of the state.

 Gray Fox

Found throughout Florida, the gray fox is a small, agile canid known for its ability to climb trees. They inhabit various habitats, including forests and suburban areas.

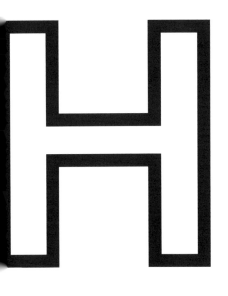 Hawksbill Turtle

A sea turtle with a distinctive hooked beak, found in Florida's coastal waters.

I

Iguana

Invasive reptile species, commonly found in Florida's warmer regions, known for its distinctive crest and spines.

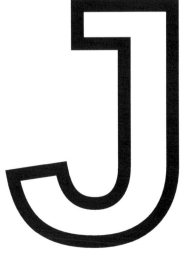

Jellyfish

Common marine invertebrates found in Florida's coastal waters, recognized for their gelatinous bodies and stinging tentacles.

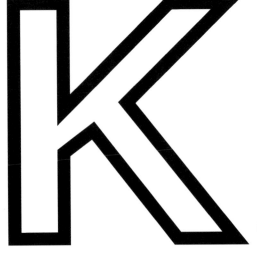

Key Deer

The smallest North American deer species, endemic to the Florida Keys, known for their petite size.

L

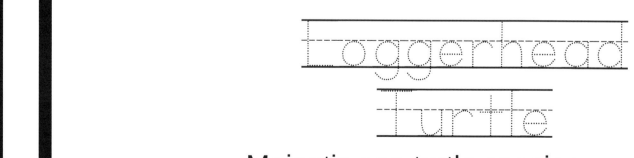

Majestic sea turtle species nesting along Florida's coasts, identified by its large head and powerful jaws.

 Manatee

Often referred to as sea cows, manatees are gentle, slow-moving marine mammals inhabitin Florida's coastal waters, rivers, and springs.

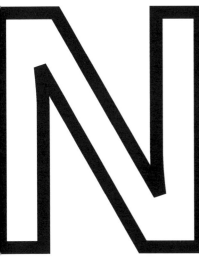

Nighthawk

The common nighthawk is a bird species found in Florida. They are known for their aerial acrobatics during dusk and dawn when hunting insects.

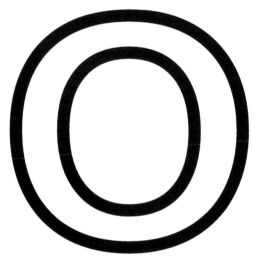 Opossum

These marsupials are common in Florida and are known for their adaptability. They can be found in urban, suburban, and rural environments.

P

Panhandle
Lizard

The Florida Panhandle is home to various lizard species, including the Eastern Fence Lizard and the Green Anole, among others.

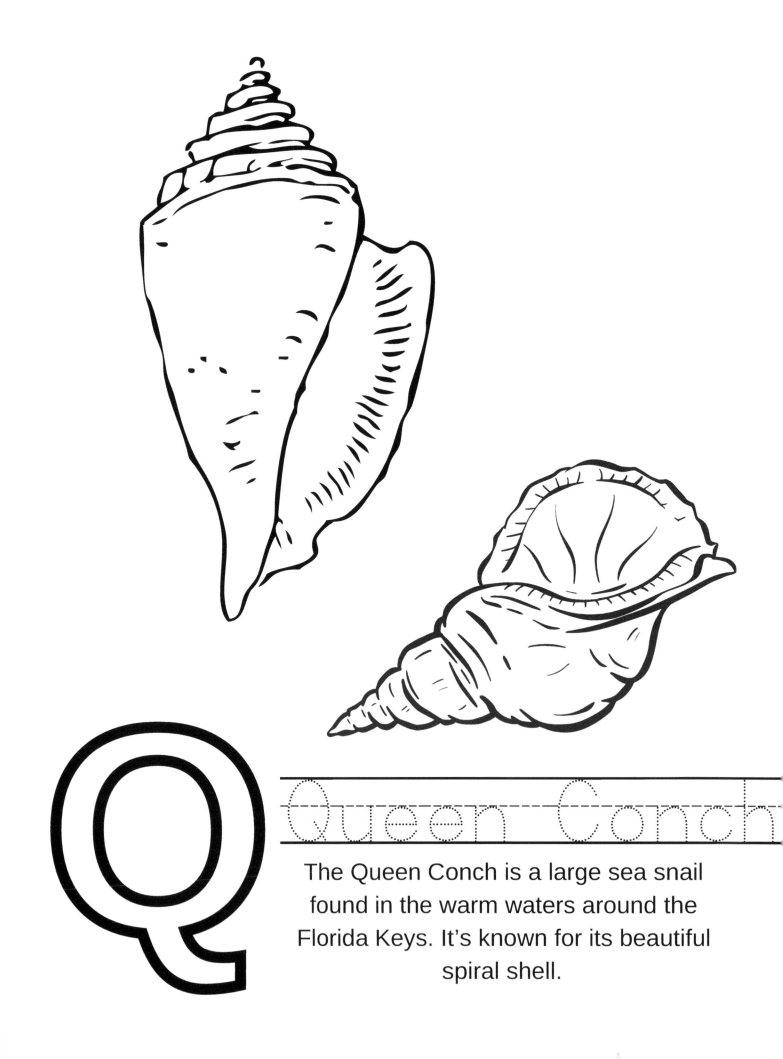

Q

Queen Conch

The Queen Conch is a large sea snail found in the warm waters around the Florida Keys. It's known for its beautiful spiral shell.

R

Roseate Spoonbill

A distinctive wading bird with pink plumage and a spoon-shaped bill. They inhabit Florida's wetlands and coastal areas.

 St. Augustine

St. Augustine is the oldest continuously occupied European settlement in the area of present day United States.

T

Tallahassee

The capital city of Florida, Tallahassee is has a rich history, beautiful oak-lined streets, and is the home of Florida State University.

U

Underwater
Caves

Florida is home to some of the most extensive underwater cave systems in the world, located mostly in the northern part of the state.

V

Vireo

A small songbird, can be found during migration seasons in wooded areas and parks of Florida.

W

Wood Stork

A large wading bird, inhabits wetlands and marshes across Florida, recognized by its distinctive bill.

Ximenez-Fatio House

Historic landmark in St. Augustine, Florida, showcasing 18th-century architecture and serving as a museum.

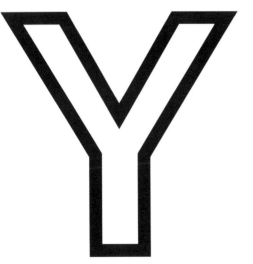 Ybor City

A historic neighborhood in Tampa, known for its vibrant culture, rich history, and Cuban influence.

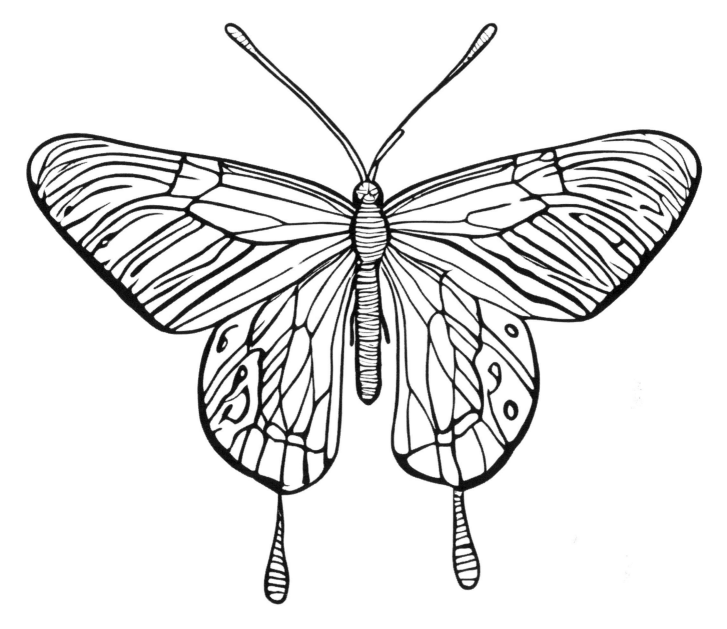

Z

Zebra Longwing Butterfly

Florida's state butterfly, identified by its black-and-yellow-striped wings, found in gardens and wooded areas.

MY COUNT TO 10 FLORIDA ANIMALS COLORING BOOK

name:

1

one opossum

2

two birds

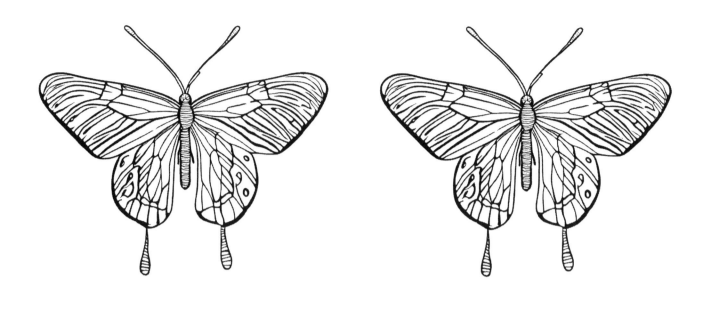

3
three butterflies

4

four iguanas

5

five storks

6

six turkeys

7
seven turtles

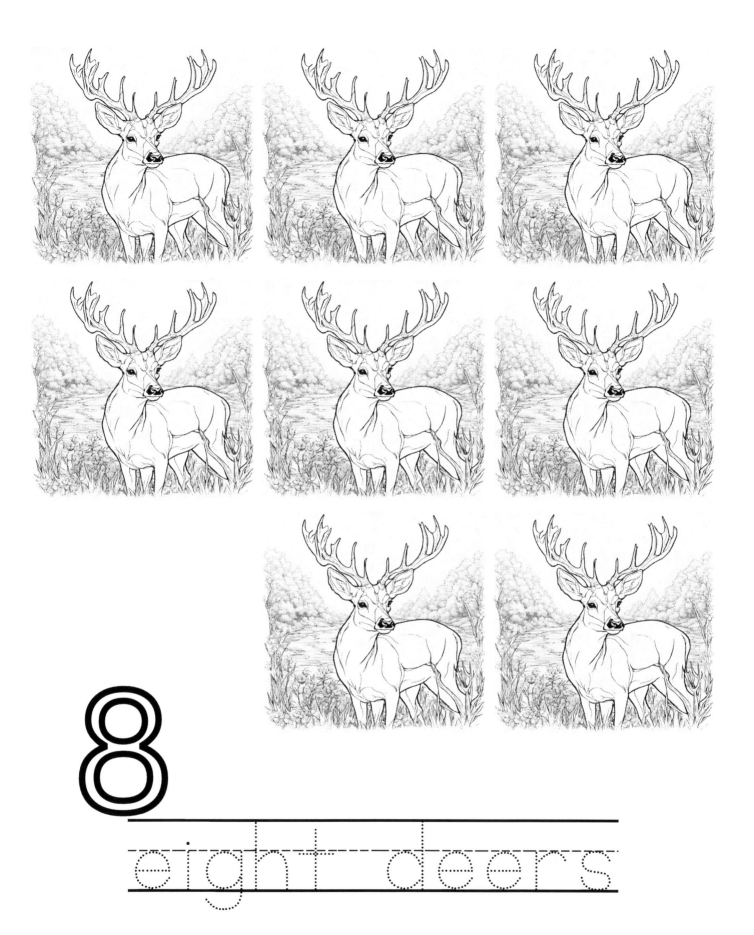

8 eight deers

9

nine panthers

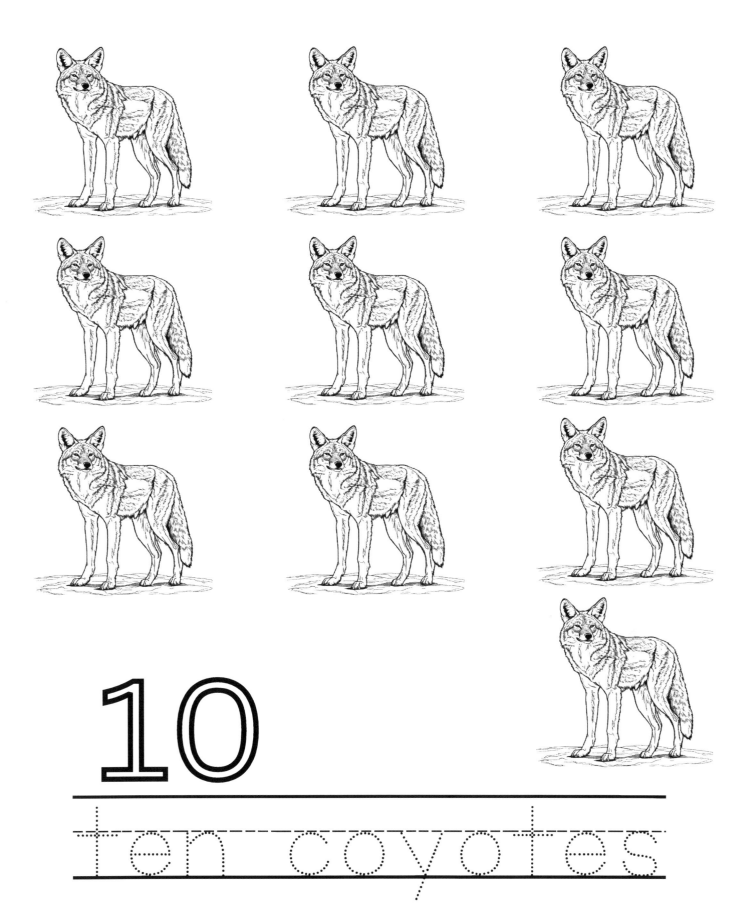

Thank you for supporting our small family business!

Learn more at:
www.LittleRedHills.com

Questions or suggestions for improvement?
Rianna@LittleRedHills.com

Wholesale order questions for your shop?
Rianna@LittleRedHills.com

Made in United States
Orlando, FL
10 September 2024